A BIT *of* SMOKE

BEN DUPREE

WESTBOW
PRESS®
A DIVISION OF THOMAS NELSON
& ZONDERVAN

WestBow Press books may be ordered through booksellers or by contacting:

WestBow Press
A Division of Thomas Nelson & Zondervan
1663 Liberty Drive
Bloomington, IN 47403
www.westbowpress.com
1 (866) 928-1240

ISBN: 978-1-4908-8540-7 (sc)

Library of Congress Control Number: 2015911241

Print information available on the last page.

WestBow Press rev. date: 08/24/2015

For Reagan and Michael:
I cannot wait to see what stories God has written for your lives.
I love you more than this page can hold.
"Children are a heritage from the Lord,
offspring a reward from him."
Psalm 127:3

Contents

Introduction

When my first book *A Dying Way of Life* was published, I was amazed at how many people enjoyed those stories about our simple yet unfortunately disappearing everyday lifestyle, about days gone by as well as the straightforward Bible lessons. So, I merely decided to dig a little deeper into that old notebook I carry in my hunting bag and continue. When those close to me questioned the title of this book, I said that I believe it could be taken a number of ways. With my love of telling stories, I have been accused on more than one occasion as merely "blowing smoke." You could also look at the tales from the past as a reminder of the brevity of our existence and how we truly are no more enduring than a puff of smoke. Whether you enjoy these stories of a simpler time or are challenged to grow spiritually during this mist we call life, I wrote this book with you in mind.

Enjoy.

Wrestling a Buffalo

During my growing-up years, my family liked to travel a lot. When I was in elementary school, my parents purchased a Palomino brand pop-up camper. Before they finally sold it to upgrade to a roomier 5th wheel, they dragged that little rolling tent all over America and crossed the Canadian border with it twice. From the screened-in windows of that little pop-up, I have witnessed the spray of the northern Atlantic as it collided with the rocks along the shores of Maine and I have heard wolves howl in the Colorado Rockies. But, out of all the destinations, Yellowstone National Park was always my favorite. The geysers, hot springs, mud pits, wildlife and unending views made an impression on this young outdoorsman. So much, in fact, that when given the chance to return during a summer break from college with my parents, brothers and sisters-in-law, I jumped at the opportunity.

The one thing you could always count on inside Yellowstone was the abundant wildlife. Many times while walking the trails between the geysers and hot springs, a resting bull elk or a meandering coyote could be spotted among the trees. Animal sightings were so commonplace, in fact, that every time we came upon a large gathering of vehicles on the side of road, we knew we were in the presence of photogenic wildlife. My tale today begins with one such creature-induced traffic jam.

We approached a wad of vehicles that apparently had been gathered long enough to alert a park ranger. While I was hoping that this particular gridlock was caused by a critter I had yet to spot, the ranger's warning came into earshot. He stood facing the road, hands raised above his head as if to form a barrier and repeatedly said with an elevated voice, "Give him some room, people. Give him some room." Excited, I peered past Ranger Rick to see whatever "him" might be. What I saw was a vast meadow (in Louisiana, we'd call it a clearing) void of trees, rocks, hills and, disappointingly enough, animals. At the far side of this expanse, a fast-moving stream created the boundary between the meadow and the jutting rock face of the opposite side.

After a few moments of rubber-necking to make sure I wasn't missing something, I asked the ranger, who was diligently trying to protect the invisible animal, "What's out there?"

"They might have seen a bear," he replied. I had yet to check "bear" off my visitor's guide of animals spotted. After a few more moments of staring at an empty field, I asked the human barricade if I could walk out there for a better look. I believe, by this time, even he was beginning to question the existence of the bear and said, "Sure. Just be careful." Unless a grizzly could manage to hide in grass barely six inches tall, I felt pretty sure I was safe. So, off I went. The prairie before me appeared flat, so with no concern for losing my bearings or becoming a victim of an ambush, I let my eyes drift to the ground. Even though this particular stop rendered no photo ops of rare-to-me beasts, I was soon caught up in admiring the beauty of this place. Wildflowers mixed with the green grass all mimicked a sea tossed by the wind. I then noticed something on the ground in the distance. There was a large, dusty, bowl-shaped area with dark brown clumps scattered all about. I had stumbled upon a buffalo wallow. The bison would roll in the dirt to obtain a protective layer of dust from the ever-present insects as well as using the earth to help them scrub off sections of their wooly winter coat. I picked up one of these clumps of hair and was immediately impressed with how thick it was. It felt as though I were holding a rug in both size and weight.

While I was studying this unusual find, I heard what every teenager dreads hearing. It was my mother's voice, calling out my name in a very public place. "Beennnn. Come baaaaack!" I could feel my face flush before I even turned around to face the bear-seekers in the parking lot. But when I did turn, I didn't see them. Thinking that perhaps I had temporarily lost my whereabouts, I quickly did a 360. It was then that I realized that the grassy acreage only appeared flat. I was at the bottom of a very subtle basin and completely out of sight from the bear-seekers. However, thanks to my mother's embarrassing barrage of commands for me to return, I had my beacon. After a few steps toward her voice, I came face-to-face with the reasoning behind my requested return. There, literally feet away, was the owner of those mats of hair. The numerous warning signs posted throughout the park alerting visitors of a buffalo's ability to sprint in speeds upwards of thirty miles per hour raced through my mind as I stared down this house with hair. Slowly, I began my retreat while expecting a charge at any moment. However, as I removed myself from his route, the buffalo ambled on to his dust bath and completely ignored me, for which I was devoutly grateful.

As I emerged from that gentle gully, I spotted my mother who was still wailing out her appeal for my hurried return. When I made my way back to the safety of our vehicle, I was approached by a young boy who looked to be about nine or ten years of age. With an excited voice, he asked, "Did you see the bear?" I had nearly forgotten about the imaginary grizzly that started this whole adrenaline rush. "No, buddy," I replied. "There's no bear out there." Then he pointed and asked "What's that?" I looked down and realized I was still holding the welcome-mat-sized chunk of buffalo hair. "Here," I said as I handed him the dusty quilt. He looked at me with huge eyes and a gaping mouth and then quickly disappeared into the cars. I walked back to my family to thank my mother for embarrassing me in front of hundreds of strangers, which was sprinkled with some fairly attractive females. Then, the young boy with his mother in tow came running up shouting, "There he is, Mom! He's the one that did it!" Confusion covered my face, I'm sure. The mother approached me in a slightly nervous, flustered manner with a confused look on her face as well. "Excuse me, but what is this?" she asked as she held out the rug I had given her son. "Buffalo hair," I replied. "How did you get it off of him?" she asked quizzically. It was at this point that my brain began to catch up. The on-lookers saw me disappear down into the valley. Then, they saw the buffalo follow me down into the dip. Then, they saw me emerge with a trophy of buffalo hair.

While suppressing laughter, I thought of what explanation this young lad must have given his mother about his recent prize. For all I knew, he believed he was in the presence of an actual buffalo wrestler. I playfully touseled the young boy's hair and while winking at him, said to his mother in my most convincing southern drawl, "Well, ma'am. It wasn't easy."

A Powerful Power Failure

The first three years of my career in education found me teaching junior high social studies at Winnfield Middle School in Winnfield, Louisiana. One of those years that has always stuck out in my memory. I had been asked to teach American history to six consecutive classes with a first hour planning period. Now, don't get me wrong. I love history. According to importance, I would rank it number one among all the studies. I said that to say this: there are only so many ways you can try to make the Monroe Doctrine interesting to eighth graders and there are only so many times you can discuss the implications of the XYZ Affair before you feel your own eyes begin to glaze over. I can tell you with certainty that number is fewer than six. So after lunch, I was beginning to feel like a worn-out tape recorder while most of the kids were just ready to go home or to sleep or both.

Now, as if teaching six hours of the exact same material weren't challenging enough, my seventh hour class presented a unique set of trials. You see this 100% male class was comprised 100% of football players who just so happened to have the P.E. class for athletes during sixth hour, the hour prior to when I had them. Their school day would end with my class. Then, they would put their pads back on and return to football practice. So, as you can imagine, not only did my room smell wonderful, but it was also slap-full of thirty-two self-proclaimed future NFL hall-of-famers whose brains I had the task of redirecting from whatever play they were about to run in fifty five minutes to how George Washington felt about foreign affairs. Not an easy chore. To the non-teacher, my best explanation is this: imagine trying to push a piece of cooked spaghetti straight uphill. It's just hard getting it all headed in the same direction.

This story deals with how blind luck stepped in and made that task much easier for the rest of the year. The bell rang for class to begin. Future Saints, Falcons and Cowboys all sprinted through my door to beat the tardy bell. It was usually quiet for twenty to thirty seconds while they caught their breath. Then, the rumbling began. Trash-talking, rehashing blown plays and bragging over successful ones were all common place as they were getting out their notebooks. Then, class began. With the season-opener right around the corner, the boys' excitement level was at a fever pitch. So, it took a little longer to get the lesson off the ground. Every time I would pause for a response to a question, gridiron gabble would revive and I would have to begin again the process of redirecting their attention.

Once I finally had the spaghetti in a fairly straight line, a lesson's worst enemy showed up. A power failure. Inevitably, this led to howls echoing down the halls as all classes derailed. With my body quartering toward the class so I could make reference to the blackboard and still face them, I waited for the initial roar to die down. Then, I turned around, placed my chalk in the tray, pointed up at the fluorescent fixtures that hung from my ceiling and for whatever reason, flatly said, "Come back on, now." Vrrrmmm. At that instant the bulbs flickered back on as the power was restored. "Now, anyway..." I said as I continued with the lesson. When I turned from writing on the board, there were thirty-two pairs of big eyes staring back at me. Somehow, I managed to keep it together.

You could have heard a mouse wrestle with a ball of cotton in that room for the rest of the class. As funny as it was for me, the icing on the cake occurred when the boys were leaving class. I overheard a defensive lineman who, even as a junior high student, already had me by an easy thirty pounds whisper to his friend, "Man, I don't care if it was a coincidence, I ain't messing up in this dude's class."

27/17

In the summer of 2006, I landed my dream job. The Natchitoches Parish School Board had voted to return the junior high students to the small elementary school in my hometown of Goldonna, Louisiana. This left them in need of a middle school math and history teacher and I was the man for the job.

I was elated to be at Goldonna for a number of reasons. First and foremost, when I accepted that teaching position, I became the third consecutive generation of the Dupree family to teach at the school at Goldonna. My father taught me when I was a student there. His brother as well as both of their parents had all had classrooms along these halls. As a matter of fact, the new scoreboard in the gymnasium was donated in honor of my father, Roy S. Dupree, and it displays the years he was principal at this fine school. He hates the attention and has said on numerous occasions that the name with the dates below it looks too much like a tombstone. He may have disliked it, but I was proud. Other reasons I was delighted to work there were the small classes, the virtual absence of anything resembling a real behavior problem and my ultra short (7/10ths of a mile) commute.

On our first day that fall of teacher meetings and room preparations, the principal, Mr. Randy Warren, called me into his office and offered me the basketball coaching job. Having never played the sport in high school, I confessed my lack of knowledge about the game hoping it would cause him to retract the offer. However, he had been a coach earlier in his career and desired to see Goldonna have its own team again. I felt relieved when he said my job was not dependent upon my taking the offer to coach and he understood if I was not interested. I thanked him for his understanding and told him I would help out any way possible with the exception of actually coaching.

As it turned out, it was a moot point. Our school census was so low that year we did not even have enough students interested to make a team. The next year, a member of the community volunteered to coach and Goldonna had a team for the first time in twenty-six years since the high school closed in 1981. Mr. Warren reminded me of my promise to help and I volunteered for crowd control. That job entailed letting the kids know what was and was not considered acceptable behavior during the games. For example, never having been to a live basketball game in their own gym, some of the children simply did not know that it was unwise to dribble their own basketball in the bleachers or to run across half court to get to the concession stand while the game was in progress. I even had to remind one Lady Wildcat it was not kosher to satisfy her craving for nachos during the game. When she asked why, I said, "Because you are our point guard!"

I made every game and I loved to watch the children try their best. During the winless season, I began to notice the boys' strengths and weaknesses. I would catch myself thinking, "If they could learn to look up and dribble, they wouldn't keep running into those traps," and "They've got to follow their shots in if they hope to get a rebound."

That next fall, Mr. Warren called me back into his office. During this conversation, he let me know the coaching offer still stood. But this time he was prepared. When he detected a decline of his offer, he said, "Look at it this way. You are already at all the games. You might as well get paid for it." Although the coaching supplement wasn't that great and I was about to discover I would actually go in the hole with all the gas I burned ferrying kids home after games and practice, I told him I would pray over it and give him an answer as soon as I had mine.

The answer came and the blessings that followed were immeasurable. Although, it took me purchasing and reading *Basketball for Dummies*, I slowly began to form a coaching plan. The areas that I noticed the previous year that needed improvement (learning to dribble while looking up, fighting for rebounds, etc.) would be my focal points. I went with a man-to-man defense simply because it was easy to teach. "See that guy? When his team has the ball, stay between him and it." I broke our offense down to the three basic positions of point guard, wing and post and explained the responsibility of each. Point brings the ball down and passes it to a wing. If a post wasn't open, the wing takes the shot and the post would block out for rebound.

One day before practice, I used this division in responsibilities as a basis of a Bible lesson. I mentioned how my favorite verse, Proverbs 27:17, states *"As iron sharpens iron, so one man sharpens another."* I then asked them a series of rhetorical questions to drive my point home. "If we had five point guards out there, who would grab rebounds? Let's assume that everybody wanted to be a post. How would the ball ever get to our end of the floor?" I then explained to the boys that by playing their position, they were making their teammates better. They were given the task of holding each other accountable on and off the floor because there were kids in their school that would kill to put that jersey on. The realization that they were now role models, whether they had asked to be or not, shocked some of them. However, this mindset, plus the fact they spent more time with each other than their own families during the season, ultimately drew them closer as a team.

On the afternoon before our first game, while we were wrapping up practice, I can recall telling the boys that all of their suicides and drills were about to pay off. I asked them not to shoot any three-pointers until the fourth quarter when we were up by at least ten points. When I made this request, I saw a light come on. They had never experienced victory before. For the first time, they believed it was possible. So possible, in fact, that their coach had planned for it.

That next evening, as we met in the team room for our prayer and a quick summary of responsibilities and scenarios, I reminded them of their duty to sharpen each other and to make each other better. As I reached for the door knob, I said "Remember, 27..." Before I could finish, they all whispered back "17." It was then I realized that these boys had heard this so much they had more than memorized it. They believed it. After their warm-ups, we met at the bench. With all hands in, they all looked at me with a mixture of excitement, fear and anticipation. I said, "No matter what, I'm proud of you boys." I realized that even though we were huddled together, I had to yell to be heard over the crowd. I said "Remember, 27." "17" came their united shouted reply. To show my excitement, I shouted even louder "27!" "17!" came their thunderous response. "Goldonna" I shouted. "Wildcats" they responded.

They took the floor that night, not as five individuals scrapping for personal glory, but rather as a team with a purpose. Although victory escaped them that night by a mere five points, they now knew it was a very real possibility, a possibility that came to reality later that week as those boys gave their town a victory for the first time in 27 years.

I coached basketball for 5 years at Goldonna Junior High School before a rare medical condition forced retirement upon me. Every season, I watched in awe as their number of wins grew and their number of defeats dwindled. During my tenure, I coached over 90 games. Before every one, the boys would remind me of their dedication by responding to my shouted number with a number of their own. "27!" "17!"

To all my Wildcats,

Matt Anderson	Josh Antee	Aaron Babers	Adrio Bailey
Major Bailey	Cody Bedgood	Justin Bedgood	Zach Bedgood
Colton Campbell	Zack Carter	CJ Comer	Aaron Conlay
Chase Cheatwood	Kurtis Garner	DJ Fairchild	Dee Franklin
Harley Godwin	Jason Jefferson	Donterius Lloyd	Jared Lonadier
Cole Meadows	Kevin Norman	Josh Page	Dennon Paul
Glen Peace	Jessie Rachal	Aaron Savell	Eddie Scallion
Jake Scallion	Cory Smiley	Tyler Sullivan	Jacob Tilley
J.T. Trichel	Tyler Trichel	Chase Walker	Dan Williams
Hunter Wilson	Brad Wise		

May you always sharpen those around you.
27/17!

A Winning Record

At Goldonna Junior High School, where I taught, we have a 30 minute session built into our schedule known as RTI (Response To Intervention). It is during this time a teacher works with a number of students grouped together by standardized test scores on one particular skill. I landed project-based mathematics. The principal suggested that since I was the boys' basketball coach and we were in the middle of basketball season, the compiling of certain basketball figures (shooting percentages, average of fouls, highest amount of points scored, etc.) would not only be beneficial but also exciting for the kids.

So we began. I gathered all the books from the previous years, which wasn't hard because we had only had a team for four years, gave them the directions for certain groups to compile certain figures and away we went. The kids loved it. I will never forget presentation day. It truly was a day of revelations.

The first child raised his hand. "Mr. Dupree, did you know that the boys' team didn't win a game until you became their coach?" I did know. Another: "Hey Coach, did you know that the boys have scored over 800 points for 2 consecutive seasons now?" I've heard that, yes. Another: "Mr. Ben, I came up with a record of 16 and 6 for the boys last year. Is that right?" You are correct. Best in school history, in fact. Still another: "Coach, it says here that we beat Fairview and Vaughn in our tournament to win the championship. Aren't they bigger than we are?" Yes. Four times our size in fact. Yet another: "Coach, this record book must be wrong. It shows Goldonna using only six boys the night we played the double-header against Fairview and Vaughn. But it also shows over twenty players got on the floor for each of them." The books are right. Six Goldonna boys outplayed forty-plus opponents that night.

Needless to say, I was glowing. The intricate details of my coaching career were laid bare and it showed success. I could hardly wait for the next hand to come up. It did. As it turned out, this was the last question of our class. And not because we ran out of time.

A cute little girl wearing glasses had been feverishly figuring up her data since class began. With her work complete, her hand shot up. "Yes, Kelsey?" was what I said. "What other information can you drop on us to reveal the awesomeness of my coaching career?" was what I was thinking. An eternity will not dull my mind of what she said next: "Mr. Ben, do you know that in the 3 years you've been coaching basketball at Goldonna that you have a losing record?" Brutal, harsh and entirely true.

More times than not, our hope for greatness proves to be an elusive creature. "One Day" statements appear in our conversations as constant reminders of the life we wished we led. One day, I'll be able to afford this, win that, lose these. It almost seems that "one day," our lives will be perfect. Sometimes those "one day" days show up on our calendar. You land that job, buy that new car, lose that weight or find that perfect someone. You marvel at what all you have amassed or have done. Then, you figure up your wins compared with your losses. This usually serves as a blunt reminder that there are several more "one day" days needed to find happiness on this Earth.

But, we can take heart in knowing that this life is not the one we were made for. If this life was all there was, then yes, it would be really easy to get depressed. But we live with the hope found in Christ Jesus that we were not made for this world. We were made by an all-knowing Creator that loved us enough, He couldn't bear the thought of spending eternity without us. So He did the unthinkable. He handed his own child over to die so that we might have a chance.

"For God so loved the world that he gave his one and only Son, that whoever believes in him shall not perish but have eternal life." We all know where the above verse comes from, but do we truly understand its power?

Remember that winning record? I finally caught it a few years ago. Had it not been for me telling the boys the significance of that win, I would have been the only person in the gym who would have known it. No celebration. No autographs. That "one day" came and went without any fanfare whatsoever. I had reached a long sought-after goal. While it did bring a brief sense of accomplishment, it also left me wondering, "Now what?" But the winning record that we find in John 3:16 has eternal glory and it is steadily growing. It puts the competition of all the other "one days" out of reach more and more each day.

So, are you still chasing "one day" perfections here on this temporary rock or have you realized your most important "one day" took place two thousand years ago?

Decide and, if I were you, I'd do it quickly. You never know what "one day" might hold.

Black "Bye"

We all have places and things that deliver us a certain level of comfort, our home field, if you will. A deer hunter may have one stand in particular with a favored weapon where he or she may feel confident and content. A golfer may have a special hole he plays with anticipation with a trusty iron. As an outdoorsman, I have many of these places and points of enjoyment. However, this story deals with the sport of bass fishing and its correlating happy place and item.

Black Bayou. Dammed up in the 1930s to create Black Lake, this narrow strip of muddy water with its shallow, sloping banks, shaded by swellbutt bald cypresses along with its gentle current almost seems as if it were created with a spinner bait (my bait of choice) in mind. Although not known for holding large fish, the "Bye" (as it is pronounced locally) was always a spot to find those little one-and-a-half-pound, tasty largemouths.

No matter where a fishing trip began, I always seemed to gravitate toward this channel. Family members and friends would chastise me for not branching out and trying new places and techniques. I would always tell them, "I've tried other places. I just like the Bye."

I fished the Bye so much, I could pretty much tell where there was going to be a fish. I can recall fishing with a buddy of mine whom I don't get to see very often. On this particular trip to the Bye, I had a pretty solid lead. We approached a cypress that had "paddles" on each side. (A paddle is a thin extension of wood at the base of the tree that is similar to a cypress knee only it is attached to the tree all the way up the trunk.) I told my buddy to throw into the pocket created by the paddle because I felt there was one laid up in there and he'll probably strike the lure as soon as it hits the water. He bounced his double willow leaf off the paddle and as soon as the skirt got wet, the fight was on. After he had the fish by the bottom lip, he looked at me and asked, "Man, how often do you fish here?" I laughed. "A lot."

Then, in the fall of 2010, a young man named Colby Hough was hired to teach physical education and to coach the girls' basketball team at Goldonna Junior High School, where I taught history, mathematics and science and coached the boys' team. One of the first conversations I had with the man dealt with the sport of bass fishing. I can recall him whipping out his phone to show me a picture of a couple of trophy bucket mouths he had landed recently. He and I coached basketball together that fall and baseball and softball together that spring. By that time, we were getting to be pretty good friends. So, one day during a P.E. class we co-taught, I asked him to look at his calendar and pick a day we could go fishing.

One evening after school that week, he and I fished the Bye. The rest, as they say, is history. Little did I know that Colby would fall in love with the Bye just as much as I had. We fished the Bye every chance we got. These fishing trips usually served as a decompressor after a long day of coaching and teaching.

It also gave us something to look forward to. You see, it was on these trips that we began to notice the elderly gentlemen that frequented the Bye. To us, these men were heroes. They were retired and could fish whenever they wanted. Bad weather or crowds didn't bother them because they could always come back tomorrow. They always knew what color to throw and were ever happy to have a conversation. Every time we left their company, one of us would say, "One day."

Colby and I fished together so often, people began to ask why we didn't fish tournaments together. But, since the average Bye bass tipped the scales at an unimpressive one-and-a-half pounds, we would respond "Oh, we would weigh in but I doubt our stringers would bring much prize money." The stories which our trips to the Bye have produced are now widely told and generally disbelieved. For example, none of our students ever believed that Colby and I saw a battleship on the Bye.

The story goes like this: We were fishing along and Colby hung his bait on an underwater snag, which was a fairly regular occurrence. We could hear a boat making its way down the channel so I decided to have a little fun. "Colby, wait until that boat gets even with us and then pretend to set the hook on a big one and let's see what happens."

The approaching boat was fairly loud and was traveling at a pretty good clip. When it rounded the bend there, as plain as day, was a large gray battleship. While not a carrier or even a destroyer, it was obviously military. It looked to be roughly thirty feet long and the driver stood on a deck which was surrounded by a rail that covered the back two-thirds of the craft. The boat was so big, in fact, that the driver had to stand up to see over the bow. When the captain peered over the vessel's cabin and saw us, he throttled down, took the boat to the far side of the Bye, turned the wheel, gunned the engine, did an impressively sharp 180 and left the premises with extraordinary speed. I lifted my sunglasses, placed them on top of my head and looked back at Colby with his bait still tangled. He just nodded his head and said, "Yeah. That just happened." Then we both burst into laughter. We've never seen it on the Bye again.

Then, one day we saw a flier for a big bass tournament that had several different divisions. For example, the bass that weighed closest to two pounds was worth $500 and the smallest bass of the day would bring in $100. When we decided to fish it, I asked Colby if he had a plan. He said, "Yeah, the Bye!" Even though we missed the $500 two-pounder by 3/100ths of a pound, we sealed the deal for the smallest when I felt a bump like a blade of grass. I reeled my bait in and was getting ready to throw again when I felt my bait wiggle.

I looked down and there hung my 0.06 pound trophy. When Colby saw how small it was, he asked, "Is that a bass?"

"I think so," I replied.

"He's smaller than the bait!" Colby exclaimed. "That's ridiculous!"

"No, buddy. That's money!" I replied. Not only did it take the bottom spot of all fish weighed in, but it was also deemed the smallest bass in that tournament's history. Not exactly how I hoped to make the record books, but I'll take it.

Yes, the Bye has produced some tales for my fishing partner and me and I'm looking forward to the day we become "heroes" ourselves.

For Colby,
"There's always the Bye."

Brotherly Competition

I have been accused on more than a dozen occasions during my life of being competitive. When my two older brothers and I get together, the spirit of competition only seems to escalate. Instead of the usual manly activities, like seeing who can burp the longest, we usually remind each other of their ownership shortcomings while boasting of our own possessions.

For example, my brother, Dan, bought a nice brick home from our parents a few years ago. I live in a triple-wide manufactured home. So, any time when bad weather threatens to roll in, Dan will usually come up with some sly comment on how my family and I can come stay at his "actual" or "sturdy" house. This usually prompts me to reply, "Are you talking about the one you bought from your Mommy?" He will usually shoot back "At least it's not portable!" to which I will usually smirk back "You know, I would probably feel the need to compensate too if I owned such a little boat." "Yours is only a foot longer!" "True. It is only a foot longer, but with 35 more horsepower." "You're just jealous that my commercial zero-turn mower can outrun your little homeowner edition." "I assume by 'commercial' that you are referring to that cute little 46-inch mower deck model. But hey, not everybody can handle the 48-inch. I believe they call that 'deck envy', Dan." "Aw, Ben. It's OK. Look on the bright side. If you ever can't find a spot at a campground for that little 25-foot 'Just-Like-Dad's' camper, you can always park it in the living room of mine." "Oh, you mean the one with that little half slide-out? You know, you sure don't see a lot of real men with those 'European editions.' I have actually heard some people refer to them as 'partial' or even 'bikini' slides. But hey, not everybody can handle a full slide. You know, like the kind I have." By the time we are done, the storm that prompted this cut-down contest has usually passed.

Our list of ammunition against each other is extensive, as I am sure by now you have surmised. It was only added to when a few years ago, we both decided to run for a city council position in our small town where the top three vote-getters were elected as Alderman. Although I thought of myself as too young and inexperienced and I figured most of the constituents would think I was not far enough removed from my little league days, I still hoped that, if I did not make the top three, Dan would not trounce me too bad. We all watched the television and wished each other luck as the results were returned. With the polls closed, the winners were projected. I can still recall the blow I felt when the anchor said, "Dan Dupree wins one of the three Village of Goldonna Alderman spots with a total of 141 votes..." My heart sank. With a community as small as Goldonna, Louisiana, 141 votes would be hard to approach. Then the anchor said "...and he was topped only by Ben Dupree with 145 votes." Eternal ammunition! Life-long bragging rights!

Then, one day while at our parents' house, Dan and I were engaged in one of our usual jabbing sessions over each others' houses and mowing decks when, out of the blue, our eldest brother, Sam, spoke up: "Children, children, please. I have a 50-inch commercial zero-turn mower and I use it to mow the yard of the brick house I built myself." Game. Set. Match. Sam.

But I still got four more votes.

For Sam and Dan,
The best brothers the world's greatest sibling could ask for.
***"A friend loves at all times, and a brother
is born for a time of adversity"***
Proverbs 17:17

21

*In all fairness, I should mention that Dan and I ran for re-election in November of 2014. We both won seats on the council. However, due to those results, my legal team and I are currently considering filing for a re-count.

A Strong Little Lady

She was baby number 13 for her parents. The cemetery already held 8 little graves in a row. The babies had been stillborn or died within a few days of birth. Today we know about blood's rH factor, but back in 1912, a tiny baby girl born 8 weeks premature at home in the dead of winter was just another tombstone to be prepared.

Things looked so bleak, the midwife didn't even tie the baby's umbilical cord. As a result, she nearly bled to death shortly after birth. Her parents, so accustomed to heartache, had not even chosen a name. The repeated losses just hurt too much. But the tiny baby survived the night, so the next morning the midwife named her Lemee--after the Lemee House on Front Street in Natchitoches, Louisiana. She wasn't given a middle name. It didn't seem necessary.

The old house was drafty and December winds can blow cold in houses heated only by a fireplace. Her mother developed an infection and ran a high fever for several days. When the midwife offered to put the baby in a separate place, her mother declined and held the dreadfully small baby close.

She always said that her mother's fever probably saved her life and served as an incubator to keep her stabilized. At any rate, the unlikely little scrap survived to become the spoiled baby of two parents (who had both been orphaned at an early age), three older sisters who doted on her and an older brother who showed his devotion by making her the target of teasing and pranks. Her growing maxed out at 5 feet 2 inches. The absence of a middle name made writing her name, Lemee Meek, easy. She would sign her school papers "LeMeek."

No one knows exactly when she became a Christian. We just know that she did. She was raised to be a lady, a decent young woman. She graduated from high school and longed to attend college, but no finances were available to make that dream come true. Whatever attracted this sweet Christian girl from Readhimer to the rambunctious, unruly, unsaved, beer-drinking young man from Goldonna, no one has ever been able to explain. But she was. And they married. And she cried and she prayed. And she threatened to leave him time and again. And he would straighten up time and again. He was scared that she meant what she said.

Two little boys were born within two years of each other. She kept praying. One day God came walking into the life of her husband-Doc Harris-and her prayers were answered. The drinking stopped immediately, but the rambunctiousness *never* did. A daughter, my mother, was added ten years later.

My mother told me of the times she can remember her Mama at the stove, and in the garden, at the wringer washing machine on the back porch, and in the barn milking cows and birthing calves. She says she can still see her stopping whatever she was doing to go hunting the bird that was making that strange call. Mamaw had spent most of her childhood in the company of Miss Caroline Dorman, an avid conservationist, so she knew every bird that was native to her homeplace (which is now *my* homeplace) and every one that was a migrant. She taught all three of her children to recognize birdcalls and to be able to tell when a jaybird had found a snake, when a cat was getting too close to the baby mockingbirds, and when the first whippoorwills and purple martins returned to our fields and houseplace in the spring.

She also taught her children to take care of folks who had less. Whether it was the elderly neighbors or missionaries on the foreign field, she did what she could to help. During the Great Depression, she along with the ladies of her church decided to set aside all the eggs that their hens laid on Sunday and sell them to raise money to support missionaries. She was faithful to her church--teaching Sunday School, Vacation Bible School, working in WMU, cooking dinner for visiting preachers and singing in the choir.

She died when she was still in her 60's--six years after burying her husband. All three of her children are Christians who serve the Lord in church; they all married Christians; all her grandchildren are Christians and they have married Christians. Even her great-grandchildren who are of age have accepted the Lord.

Papaw Doc put the fizz in their lives, but Mamaw Mae was the rock. She anchored them all. Her unfailing faith and trust in God are why on any Sunday morning there are folks in church in Goldonna, Ruston, Deridder, and Baton Rouge, Louisiana; Dallas, Texas, and someplace in Missouri. When you have faith the size of a mustard seed--when you're not much bigger than a mustard seed yourself--God has promised He will hear and He will bless.

Lemee Meek Harris
December 22, 1912-October 26, 1982

This story, largely told to me by my mother, is about a woman who appears in one of my earliest memories. I only wish I could recall more. However, one day that won't matter.

Guinea Eggs and Little Sisters

Guineas, or guinea-fowl, as they are known in the South, were a commonly-owned and useful animal. Not only did they serve as wonderful table fare and excellent guard dogs, they also come in handy to any family who owns chickens. You see, guinea eggs have an extremely durable shell. I've been told that you can throw them at a pine tree and they will just merely bounce off. This truth, coupled with the fact that a guinea egg is speckled, oblong in shape and impossible to confuse with a chicken egg, is why they prove valuable to any keeper of barnyard fowl. You see, a guinea egg would be placed in the nesting box of the chickens as a nest egg, which was used for coaxing the hens into laying in that box. Once the hens began laying eggs it was always easy to distinguish between the hen egg and that of a guinea. After a time of service, since the guinea egg didn't hatch, it would inevitably spoil and need to be disposed of.

My grandparents, Doc and Lemee Harris, lived on the same property I do now. They raised many animals on my hill, including chickens, and their corresponding guineas. One day, Mamaw Mae told her oldest son, Glynn, to dispose of a rotten guinea egg by taking it out in the woods behind the house and busting it to ensure a dog did not decide to bring it back. Glynn was obedient. As he was walking across the yard, he playfully tossed the egg to his younger brother, Tom. Before long, a game ensued. After each toss, the catcher would back up a few steps and let the rotten egg fly again.

Once Glynn had the egg in his possession, he decided since he was the oldest, he would see to it this game ended in his favor.

As he was preparing to crow-hop into the throw, Tom caught wind of his plan. Tom stayed still until the spoiled sphere was airborne. Then, Tom quickly darted out of the flight path. Unbeknownst to both of the boys, little sister Linda had followed Tom to see what the boys were up to. Glynn's moldy missile was right on the mark. The only problem was the target had moved and the rock-hard, repulsive egg splattered right between the curious blue eyes of little sister, Linda. The wailing commenced.

As Tom, gagging, tried to clean her off, Glynn noticed the crying had alerted Mama. With Mae, mad as a hornet, storming their direction Glynn did, in my opinion, what was some pretty quick thinking. When Mae demanded to know what had happened to her baby, Glynn-- the launcher of the guinea egg--proudly announced, "Tom let her get hit!" While desperately trying to clean up his little sister, Tom looked guilty enough. While I'm not sure what punishment followed, I can only assume it was severe for my Uncle Tom and avoided by my Uncle Glynn. I say this because when Uncle Tom told me this story about my mother taking a rotten guinea egg to the forehead, he jokingly entitled it "Why I Hate your Mother."

May 19, 2014 holds no red text on anyone's calendar. However, the importance of this day cannot be overstated for me. For on this random Monday, I took my own advice, interrupted my schedule and sat down and listened as my Uncle Tom spun yards from days gone by. Little did I know that this was the last time I would see him on this Earth. *"People leave this world and they often do it without warning. Don't let the past die with its generation."*

Uncle Tom,
That was an amazing day. I cannot fathom how much fun we'll have in Paradise. I'll meet you at the gate.
Thomas Roy Harris
July 8, 1939-April 30, 2015

A Family Full of Failures

I once saw a church sign that read "If your church were perfect, you couldn't be a member." That got me to thinking about how the world sees us Christians. We follow the perfect being, The Christ, the One the scriptures tell us that no deceit was found in his mouth. So naturally the world believes that we should be perfect, and it loves to point out the mistakes of Christians and challenge our beliefs publicly. Think about any time a Christian has publicly stood up for Christ. Mel Gibson made the film "Passion of the Christ" and later divorced his wife and was pulled over for a DUI. Miss California stood up for the institution of marriage. Shortly thereafter, nude pictures of her surfaced. This resulted in the loss of her crown. We're not perfect. So, let's look at Christianity for what it really is: A family full of failures. That's what we are. If there is one who can honestly say they have never failed then he or she doesn't need Christ. But we all know that such a human being does not exist because scriptures tell us that all have failed and fallen short. Perhaps we will see that it's not such a bad thing after all. God can turn even our failures into positives. Let's look at 3 positive points about failure.

1. Humility

The first positive thing about failure is that it teaches us humility. The best example I can think of is found in the individual of Peter. He grew so powerful in his own head, that pride took root. Jesus recognized this, and spoke of it to him. Luke 22:31-32 says, ***"Simon, Simon, Satan has asked to sift you as wheat. But I have prayed for you, Simon, that your faith may not fail. And when you have turned back, strengthen your brothers."***

But Peter's immediate and prideful response was in verse 33, ***"Lord, I am ready to go with you to prison and to death."***

Satan wanted to crush Peter like wheat. What he hoped to find in the rubble was simply chaff, which could be easily blown away. But Jesus assured Peter that his faith, although it would falter, would not be destroyed. Satan did crush him. Jesus did reinstate him and Peter took to the ministry with a different perspective. He was now humble enough to lead others and help them in their own time of being crushed by Satan. To show you the flip side of this, let's look at Judas.

Judas was another that was crushed by Satan. Peter denied and Judas betrayed. One act is just as wrong as the other. But these two men had entirely different fates simply because one of them repented.

2. Sympathy

The second good thing about failure is that it teaches us sympathy. There is an excellent chance that regardless whatever you are going through in your life right now, there is someone that you know and trust who has already dealt with the same problem. The flip side of that is that there is probably someone in your life who is struggling with something similar to what you have dealt with before. God gives us these opportunities so we can feed off of each other, sharpen each other, and pray for each other. We are in this together.

Who does a Christian have to interact with or to draw strength from? The world? The media? No. We simply have each other. First Corinthians 12:26 says, ***"If one part suffers, every part suffers with it. If one part is honored, every part rejoices with it."*** We need each other. You need someone and someone needs you. Let our failures draw us closer together to support, love and learn from one another. Again, my favorite passage of scriptures fits in perfectly here. Proverbs 27:17 says, ***"As iron sharpens iron, so one man sharpens another."***

3. God's grace

The third good thing about failures is that they teach us the depth of God's grace. Let me ask you: "Is anyone beyond God's reach? Is anyone beyond repair?" The answer is no. From the pulpit of my home church, I have heard from such people as Jack Daniels, who was a horrible alcoholic and Jack Hollingsworth, who tried to drink himself to death. I have heard of a young man who was so involved in drugs that he buried friends that did smaller amounts of cocaine than he did, and another young man is alive on this earth today because his mother was raped when she was thirteen years of age.

Jack Daniels is now a wonderful evangelist preaching the gospel. Jack Hollingsworth is now part of the Acts 29 Ministry that travels our country full time spreading the word of Christ. The first young man is now a college student and a guitarist for a professional Christian band and the second young man is a preacher and the lead singer in that same band because his grandmother believed that God knew best and instead of choosing not to have a child they never asked for, she raised that child in the name of Christ. Either God can erase *all* sin or He cannot erase any. The level of God's grace that I've seen tells me that no failure is too great for God to overcome.

I can recall hearing an opposing basketball coach shouting at his team that failure was not an option. Well, Coach, I hate to break it to you, but failure is part of life (and for you it was about to be part of that game!) The question is "What are you going to do about it?" or better yet, "What are you going to let God do with it?"

So, the next time someone, whether that individual is Satan or a fellow human being, points out your failures, just smile and reply, "I know I'm not perfect. My brothers and sisters know I'm not perfect. But I serve a God that can still use a failure such as I am to bring about his grace."

Don't let Satan or anyone make you think you are unworthy of God's love because of your past. I would like to share with you one of my favorite sayings: "When the devil reminds you of your past, remind him of his future."

Memories of Holiday Traditions and Those Yet to Come

I can remember coming in from duck hunting Thanksgiving morning and seeing Mama in the kitchen making dressing while several pecan pies cooled on the counter. I can remember the smell of turkey and cranberry sauce as I entered my grandmother's house later that same day. I can remember popping fireworks in our yard on Christmas Eve while sipping hot chocolate. I can remember how my grandmother would sit and laugh at her grandsons while we ran from the sputtering fuses. I can remember listening for the sound of reindeer hooves on the roof of my house. I can remember bounding down the hall in the predawn hours to see the only light coming from the radiant Christmas tree protected by a ring of presents which were proof that Saint Nick had crept in during the night. I can remember gazing upon my grandmother's white porcelain Christmas tree while wondering how Santa always knew where my Mamaw lived. I can remember choking down black-eyed peas and cabbage at dinner on New Year's Day while she explained how it was only the proper thing to do.

Needless to say, the holidays have always held a significant portion of my heart. The traditions I can recall still exist in my family today. We added a few loved ones to the gatherings with each marriage and birth and we've lost a few with each death. But neither births nor deaths can stop the holiday tradition. Those family members that have gone on to be with the Lord are just as much a part of our get-togethers now as when they were alive. They are spoken of fondly as the memories are tossed about. At times during the conversation one could almost declare that Papaw was just in the back room lying down after the meal as he always did.

The faces around the table change. Some disappear from one year to the next while new ones appear in their mother's arms. No matter what changes, one thing never fades away: the tradition will remain.

In my meager opinion, the calendar does not make these times of year special. They are made special by the sacred rituals that we attach to them. During these times of the year, it is important to focus on the gifts from the Lord that you hold dear, not what the world tells you is important. Remember those that have left this world, and live your life in such a way as to make those who come after you have just as many fond memories of your time on the Earth. I believe those memories will hold us over until they can be experienced again for an eternity with our family, seated at the holiday table of our Christ.

Romans 8:28

Romans 8:28 is one of the most memorized, beloved, quoted scriptures of all time. To the Christian, its importance and relevance is rivaled only by the promise found in John 3:16. However, Romans 8:28 is also one of the most misquoted and misunderstood verses of the Bible.

Romans 8:28 says, "**And we know that God causes everything to work together for the good of those who love God and are called according to his purpose for them.**" It does NOT say "God causes everything to work out the way I want it to" or "God promises us all a happy ending here on Earth."

The last time I checked, we live in a fallen world. Only in Heaven is everything perfect. Everything is perfect there because his will is always done. That is why in the Lord's Prayer we say, "Thy will be done on Earth as it is in Heaven." But we all know that it is not. It is not the Lord's will that any should fall away, but they do. The reason the Lord's will is not done on Earth as it is in Heaven is because Earth is a fallen world. Heaven is not.

So, I would like for you to take a gander with me at Romans 8:28 phrase-by-phrase. I would like to take it apart piece by piece and maybe along the way, we can discover and grasp its true meaning.

"We know"

This is not a positive attitude nor is it looking at the glass half full. This could not even be classified as wishful thinking. This is an example of absolute certainty based on truth and faith. We don't think. We don't hope. We don't guess. We know. "Know what?" some may ask. That God is real and in control. Period.

"that God causes"

God is the grand designer. A person asked me one time to prove that God is real. I took off my wristwatch. Then I told him, "There's quite a story behind this watch. I went to all the fine jewelry stores in town and bought the best I could afford, all of the hundreds of moving parts from the gears and hands to the hinge and buckle, as well as the leather strap, face and crystal. Even though I had spent all that time gathering up all the pieces, the watch was totally disassembled. No part was touching another. So, I put the parts into a shoe box, duct-taped it shut and vigorously shook the box for a couple of hours. Then, when the box was opened, inside I found a fully assembled wristwatch with not only the correct time down to the second, but also the correct date." Then I asked the person, "Do you believe me?" A doubting smirk and a shaking head were his reply. "Which is easier to believe," I asked, "that this wristwatch fell together by chance or that somebody put it together?"

He looked at me like I was crazy. He said, "Of course someone put that watch together. You could shake that box for a million years and it would never create a watch, much less one with the correct time and date."

I said, "Exactly. Isn't it easier to believe that God took all of these elements and created life than it is to believe we all just happened by chance?"

If the Earth's axis were tilted one degree closer to the sun, the temperature of our atmosphere would reach a level that could not sustain life. If it were one degree farther away from the sun, we would ultimately freeze. If our atmosphere had one percent more oxygen, we would explode the first time somebody caused a spark. Some of the most brilliant minds of today that are involved in such complex things as theoretical physics and applied mathematics have been quoted as saying, "There is nothing random." And some of these are even atheist. We may mess up from time to time. God never does. He cannot. He is God.

"everything"

Everything. All that has happened to you: your hurt, your failures, your sins, illnesses you or a loved one have dealt with, insurmountable debt you've faced, a divorce that tore your family apart, heartbreak, death of someone close. God is able to bring good out of the worst of evil. If you don't believe that, look at what he did at Calvary. He did it once for every human. Do you believe he can do it in your life?

"to work together"

Not separate nor independent. Together. Everything in our lives working together. Our successes as well as our failures. Our standing ovations as well as when we wish we had a rock to crawl under. Think of it as a cake. Raw eggs, salt, and flour are found in one's ingredients. Now, if I laid out raw eggs, salt, and flour before you, you probably wouldn't be too anxious to dig in. Why? Because separately, they are unpleasant and distasteful. However, when you mix them all together, they become something delicious. This part tells us to give God all of your distasteful, unpleasant experiences and He will blend them. This will lead us to our next point.

"for the good"

Let's make this clear. It does NOT say, "Everything will be good." This is where most people misquote and misunderstand this verse. There is a lot of bad in our world. But God specializes in bringing good out of the bad. Let's take a look at one family's history. One young woman in this family wanted to have a baby so badly that she seduced her father-in-law to get pregnant. Another was an openly-practicing prostitute. Another woman in this family tree was an outlaw, broke a major law and showed no respect for authority. Another woman cheated on her husband, got pregnant and stood by as her boyfriend killed her husband and did nothing to stop it. What good could come out of a family as twisted and horrible as this? Before we go any further, beware. The answer may shock you. The people I've just described to you are found in the Bible and are all ancestors of Jesus Christ. Tamar seduced her father-in-law for the sole purpose of getting pregnant. Rahab was a prostitute. Ruth was not Jewish and broke the law by marrying a Jewish man. Bathsheba committed adultery with David and then sat quietly by as David had her husband killed. Yet through these flawed individuals, through these horrible sinners, God brought about perfection. He brought about the Christ Jesus.

"of those who love God and are called"

Here we find a promise. A promise just for us. A promise just for the Christian. God's children only. We are those that love God and obey his commands. We're not perfect. We are just simply forgiven. For the rest of the world it could be said that all things work for evil. But not us.

"according to His purpose for them."

"What purpose?" you may ask. So that we may become *"like His Son,"* which we find in the following verse, 8:29. Try to think of something in your life that you wish had not happened to you. I don't know about you, but I did not have to think for very long. But then stop and think that everything God allowed to happen in your life is for the purpose of making you like His Son, Jesus Christ. To be like Christ is our ultimate goal here on earth. Sounds simple, right? However, we must realize that he learned obedience through the things he suffered. So must we.

So, after reading and contemplating this beloved verse, I hope it holds even more importance for you. I hope we all truly understand its meaning, honestly grasp its significance and faithfully rely on its promise. Today, I now pray that we all know God as the great designer who uses everything, the good and the evil, to extend his kingdom and uses it for the ultimate good of those he calls his children.

Lightning Bugs

Growing up in a Christian home, I learned to recite John 3:16 as one of my early mottos. At Vacation Bible School every summer, these words were quoted at the beginning of each service, right along with the pledges to the Holy Bible, Christian flag and American flag. It is a verse beloved by Christians the world over. *"For God so loved the world that he gave his one and only Son, that whoever believes in him shall not perish but have eternal life."* It holds the very basis of the Christian faith--a father who loved his own creation enough that he could not bear the thought of eternity without it. So, He allowed the death of His son in order that we might have the opportunity to develop a relationship with Him on this side and secure an eternity in His presence on the other.

While this provision is nothing short of awesome, God's love for us is still much deeper than most of us will ever realize. Allow me to share with you an iota of God's affection that has recently been brought to my attention. Let me ask, have you ever seen a lightning bug (aka firefly)? Good. Now, have you ever stopped to cogitate on what's up with this regular looking, run-of-the-mill bug that has been endowed with a glow-in-the-dark rear end? Now, I am certain that modern science could provide us with ample reasoning (ranging from finding a mate to flickering out some entomologic Morse code) as to why these little airborne blinkers light up our summer night skies.

Forgive me, but I believe a lightning bug's ability to emit a soft glow serves a much deeper purpose. Could it be that the Almighty placed this little creature in our lives for the sole purpose of making us smile? I can just see Him on the day scheduled for the creation of all insects when the specs for this one little harmless flying beetle came across His workbench. He grinned as He endowed this little dude with a flashing rear and thought to Himself "The kids are gonna love this!"

Upon creation of our world, our Father gave us everything we need to survive. But I also believe He created some things just to show He loves us. The sun could rise and set without that vast array of colors. The ocean did not have to be such a vibrant blue as it broke over the contrasting white sand of the beach. The azalea bloom did not have to give off such a delicate fragrance. But they all do. Our topic of discussion fits in nicely here.

I have fond lightning bug memories from my childhood. I can remember chasing these little floating light bulbs in my front yard while my parents sat on the porch, giggling at me and my two older brothers. I now have the opportunity to do the same with my children on that same hill.

As I have previously stated, I believe God created this world with so much more than is needed to simply sustain life. He does not want us to merely survive. He desires that we thrive. He wants us to enjoy His handiwork. If we do, then a lightning bug has a purpose after all. It reminds us of a creative, loving, seeking God that loves you so much, he would paint the rear end of a bug just to see you smile.

Doc and the Panther

My maternal grandfather was Mr. Thomas Ernest "Doc" Harris. He was the supervisor of predator control and the head trapper for the Department of Wildlife and Fisheries for the state of Louisiana. Back then, just as today, legends and rumors of a wild panther ran rampant across north Louisiana. Missing or half-eaten livestock around the Provencal, Louisiana (pronounced *Pra-ven-saw*) community gave credibility to the rumors. In fact, so many complaints were filed in the Red Dirt area in southern Natchitoches Parish, the LDWF dispatched Doc to trap the nuisance animal. Since the commute between the villages of Goldonna and Provencal was rather lengthy, he stayed with local families, one being Mr. Led O'Bannon, while he studied the animal. People always said that Doc, like any good trapper, had the ability to think like the animal he was pursuing.

After a few days, he had the cat's haven pin-pointed. He and his youngest son, Tom, set their traps in a sandy ravine that Doc figured the cat was using as a discreet traveling route between feeding areas. (This style of trap was triggered when a creature stepped onto a flat metal disk called a pan. Dirt and leaves were removed from beneath the pan to create a hollow spot. The debris that was removed from under the pan was then sprinkled on top of it to serve as camouflage. The animal would step on the pan and it would sink into the vacant hole below far enough to trigger the jaws of the trap.) A hard rain that evening served to wash away any human scent in the area and

Tom and Doc awoke the next morning confident. As they were headed out, Doc expressed his faith in the day's excursion. "I've got a good feeling about this morning," he said. "What are we going to do with that panther if we catch it, Daddy?" Tom asked. Tom then was shown a side of his father he did not see very often. Doc's face displayed a mixture of uneasiness and remorse. "Son, if we catch it, we will have to put it down." Doc paused before he continued. "I hate to do that because it could very well be the only one in this neck of the woods."

As they approached the trap, their high hopes for the morning took a nose dive. There was the trap, still perfectly set and undisturbed. Upon closer examination, Doc discovered that the hard rain the night before had washed sand into the void beneath the trap's pan, thereby making it impossible for the trap to function. The deluge also covered the pan with moist sand over an inch deep. But right there, in the middle of the pan, was a perfect panther print. When they noticed it, Tom saw a look that was comprised of success, relief, and pride come across Doc's face. He had outsmarted the animal; his instinct was proven correct. But, he didn't have to end the animal's life and was blessed with a souvenir that would come to have quite the storied past.

Doc made a plaster cast of the print and, being quite the prankster, he got plenty of use from it. Anytime he was in close proximity to wet concrete, he felt it was his divine duty to bestow the cement with the track of that panther. When my parents built a large brick house next door to Papaw Doc's place, the panther strolled across their front porch and appeared to enter their front door. When the foundation of Goldonna Baptist Church was poured, the panther made it a point to step just beneath the right front window. I now live where Papaw Doc's house used to be. His front walkway that he ambled up every evening after work still graces my yard. A few years ago I was spraying some grass and weed killer around various mowing obstacles in my yard. There was an old filled-in well head that had been concreted into the ground. Even though I had mowed over it for years, I doused it with poison mainly to see how big around that thing really was. After the next mowing had knocked away all the dead grass, I was walking across my yard and something caught my eye. There in the cement collar of Doc's old well was the print of the panther. I can't help but wonder how many more are out there.

Although not immortalized in concrete, I do know of another instance where the panther track caused quite a stir. Near the village of Provencal, Louisiana, there was a cave back in the red clay hills. A lady whose family had provided Papaw Doc with room and board had told me that everyone always referred to it as the Wolf Cave. With the stories, rumors and sighting of panthers throughout the area in full swing, Doc took it upon himself to have a little fun with the plaster print. He made it appear as though the evasive creature had traipsed right up into the cave but yet mysteriously never left. The lady told me after the tracks were discovered, the cave's name changed from the Wolf Cave to the Panther Cave. While I can find evidence to neither support nor destroy this theory, I do find it peculiar that the school at Provencal settled on the panther as its mascot. I can't help but wonder how many miles and through how many lives that old panther strolled.

Papaw,

Even though we never had the opportunity to meet on
this Earth, you definitely left your print on me.
T.E. "Doc" Harris
March 5, 1909-February 19, 1976

Spare Tires and Bobcats

During my grandfather's, Doc Harris, tenure as head trapper for the state of Louisiana, the bobcat was always the one beast that most often found its way into Doc's traps. The reason being was that the bobcat not only threatened the calves of cattle farmers along the various rivers, but they also were a major threat to the whitetail deer fawn. Wolves, dogs and coyotes hunt primarily with their sense of smell. Newborn deer, however, are odorless. But, for the bobcat, who hunts by sight, they were an easy prey. With the Louisiana Department of Wildlife and Fisheries trying desperately to establish a whitetail population in North Louisiana, Doc was often dispatched to trap these spotted felines.

One day, Doc got a call from the zoo in Alexandria, Louisiana. They were in need of a native Louisiana bobcat and the LDWF put them in touch with the man for the job. A few days later, he trapped a healthy specimen near the town of Jonesboro, Louisiana. Doc and his son, Tom, loaded the bobcat into the back of their old Willis Jeep. With a foot still in the trap and a choker (a long metal pipe which contained a long flexible cable looped at one end that could be tightened) around its neck, they carefully loaded the upset critter, known for its long needle-like teeth and razor sharp claws, into the back of the jeep.

They didn't have the luxury of a kennel of any sort. So, they just wedged the choker in such a manner that secured the cat in place.

However, due to the length of the choker, they were forced to leave the back glass and tailgate open to make room. They loaded up and off to Alexandria they went. The 50 mile road trip was a fairly rare occurrence back in those days and they both looked forward to it. They laughed and joked as they bumped their way down the road. At some point, Doc asked Tom, "How's our bobcat doing?" When Doc didn't get an immediate reply, he looked at Tom, who was staring wide-eyed back at his father.

Doc spun his head around to discover what Tom had already caught wind of. The cat was gone. As Doc uttered "con-found" (his ultimate "things-have-gone-awry" statement), Tom decided to look out the window to see if the cat's exit had been a fairly recent event. On a Willis Jeep, the spare tire was mounted just behind the passenger side door. So, when Tom leaned out, he instinctively braced himself on the tire. However, his search didn't take very long. There, nose-to-nose with Tom, crouched on the spare tire, with the trap and choker still firmly in place, was one very irate, windblown bobcat. The sudden encounter startled Tom to the point that he jumped into his father's lap while he was driving. I wish I could have been there to determine who was more surprised, Tom when he found himself nose-to-nose with a ticked-off cat or Doc when he found his teenage son in his lap while driving 60 miles per hour.

The Story of a Skeptic

I have always enjoyed studying the various characters that appear in the scriptures. Just like believers today, these individuals came from differing backgrounds and a wide array of geographic locations. I always find it interesting to discover what lessons may lie just underneath the surface in the lives of these varied personalities. There is one particular person that I am willing to bet you will be able to identity simple by his man-given nickname: *Doubting* _____ (fill in the blank).

Yes, poor Thomas has been saddled with a label that has stuck for centuries. He walked, ate, listened, learned and even witnessed miracles in the presence of the most influential man planet Earth has ever seen. Yet, he has gone down in history as a doubter. He has been called everything from a skeptic to a rationalist to the prototype of the Rational Argument. He's a "see-it-to-believe-it" kind of guy. The tragic part is that, throughout the history of Christianity, he is viewed with almost the same disdain as Judas.

They both lived with Jesus and with disbelief. Figuratively speaking, when their moment of truth arrived, they lied. Hopefully, we will soon see Thomas in a different light. Instead of shunning him and keeping him on the dark side of Christian history, I believe we should study his life and his decisions. If we take time to wipe away all the man-made "dirt" that has been slung at him throughout centuries, what we will find may not only help us grow in our walk with Christ, but may also enable us to catch the familiar glimpse of ourselves in his reflection during the cleaning process.

I always like to begin my scripture-character profile with a little background information. With Thomas, this is fairly easy because there isn't any. While he is mentioned in the first five books of the New Testament, he is found only in a list in all but the book of John. John 11:16 says, *"Then Thomas (also known Didymus) said to the rest of the disciples, 'Let us also go, that we may die with him.'"* This brave declaration was made after Jesus told the twelve he was planning on visiting Judea, a place where he had recently barely avoided a stoning. So, we can safely surmise that Thomas was sold out to Jesus at this point, even to the point of death.

Thomas pokes his head up again in verse five of chapter fourteen: *"Thomas said to him, 'Lord, we don't know where you are going, so how can we know the way?"* Jesus' answer is the very backbone of Christianity, *"I am the way and the truth and the life. No one comes to the father except through me."* Thomas displayed the same misunderstanding about Jesus that the disciples displayed all too often. When reading this scripture, I find myself wondering, "How could Thomas not have understood this?" Then, I must remember that we've had roughly 2,000 years to read, dissect and study these words. These twelve men were hearing them for the very first time and reacted in the same manner I believe most of us would.

Then after the death and resurrection of Jesus, Thomas makes another appearance. Verses 24 and 25 of chapter 20 show us a broken-hearted, distraught man. *"Now Thomas (called Didymus), one of the Twelve, was not with the disciples when Jesus came. So the other disciples told him, 'We have seen the Lord!' But he said to them, 'Unless I see the nail marks in his hands and put my finger where the nails were, and put my hand into his side, I will not believe it.'"* Then verses 26-28 happened. *"A week later his disciples were in the house again, and Thomas was with them. Though the doors were locked, Jesus came and stood among them and said, 'Peace be with you!' Then he said to Thomas, 'Put your finger here; see my hands. Reach out your hand and put it into my side. Stop doubting and believe.' Thomas said to him, 'My Lord and my God!'"* Jesus knew exactly what it would take for Thomas to believe and he gave it freely. There was no rebuke, berating nor reproach. Instead, Jesus said "Peace…see…reach out." He went to work on Thomas right away.

Thomas' faith needed rebuilding. Once upon a time, Thomas had believed all was good. Then, the unthinkable happened. He watched as Jesus--his Savior--was beaten, nailed to a cross, taken down and buried in a tomb. He saw a huge rock separating him from his light forever, as far as his mind could fathom.

This particular juncture of Thomas' story reminds me of a story I heard an old pastor tell. One day, Satan decided to go out of business. So he had a yard sale with all of his tools he would no longer need. Hatred, Envy, Jealousy, Deceit, Lust. They were all laid out on display with their price tags. At the end of the table, there was one small harmless-looking tool which showed signs of lots of wear. However, this little tool was priced higher than all the rest combined. When asked what it was, Satan replied, "Disappointment."

Someone asked "Why so expensive?"

Satan then said, "Because, it is more useful to me than all the others."

Has dealing with disappointments made you question the validity of your relationship with God? When our walk with Christ is a sunny stroll, life is good. But when the lightning of trouble or despair strikes, do we continue on our path or dive for cover?

I have discovered that when I begin to feel like Thomas and I need God to "prove" how much he loves me, he does it in a variety of ways. I can recall a day early in my teaching career that I knew in advance was going to be a long one. I had papers to grade. I had a full schedule of preparing nearly 200 junior high students for state testing. Top that off with a faculty meeting and then a 4-hour parent teacher conference after the school day came to an end and I had the making of a stressful day. I even left home earlier than usual that morning to give myself more time to prepare. As I was driving down the road at this unusual time, I was praying. I can remember saying, "Lord, you know how long today is going to be. I'm going to need your strength to make it because I don't believe I can do it on my own." I had no more said these words when I rounded a bend into a straight stretch of eastbound highway. There before me was the most beautiful, radiant sunrise I had ever seen.

Had I left for work at my usual time, I would have missed this extravagant masterpiece. I could feel God's love as he flooded me with his grace and compassion. I could hear Him as he spoke to me through that dawn. "My child, if I can create this, don't you think I can handle your day?" That day was tough. It was over a decade ago and I remember it still. But, I survived.

So, the next time disappointment clouds your view of God's love for you, pray that he would open your eyes to whatever way he decides to use to show you his hands and his side. Listen to whatever courier he sends to deliver the beautiful message: "Peace be with you, my child. Here's proof. I'm alive. I'm here. I will never leave you no matter how much you doubt."

Defeat

I'm a history teacher by trade and I have always been drawn to the different wars in which our country has been engaged and how the beginning, course and conclusion of a war had the ability to shape and even define a generation. One war I've always wanted to study more about was World War II.

Both of my grandfathers served in the U.S. Navy. My paternal grandfather, John A. Dupree, was a Navy medic on a destroyer during D-Day, June 6, 1944. The tales of his ship's constant bombardment of the beach were gruesome enough. Up until the time Gen. McArthur ordered the storming of the beach, the outcome of the war was uncertain. Victory was hoped for but not guaranteed. After this fateful day, in which an estimated 10,000 people gave their lives, it was obvious that we would win the war. That doesn't mean that life was peachy in the day-to-day trenches, but the grand outcome was no longer in question.

America pulled off an impressive feat by fighting on two separate fronts simultaneously: Europe and the South Pacific. The Pacific front had a D-Day of its own when America dropped the atomic bomb on Hiroshima on August 9, 1945. The Allied forces claimed victory of World War II on September 2, 1945, as Japan was the last enemy to surrender. This day became known as V-Day.

In between these dates, Japan got desperate. They began what became known as the kamikaze attacks. Kamikaze attacks consisted of Japanese fighter pilots flying their warplanes, loaded with fuel and explosives, into American warships.

Their "Death before Defeat" tactics appeared weak and pathetic to the on-looking world. News outlets covering the attacks bragged that these desperate acts were only 14% successful. With a navy larger than the combined forces of all other combatant nations at the time, America lost a grand total of 47 ships to kamikaze attacks with 300 suffering damage.

The Japanese knew there was no chance of victory so they turned to terrorism to slow down and frustrate the victor. This was the act of a defeated enemy.

However, try to imagine what the sailors on those 47 doomed ships felt like. To them, the Japanese won. The Japanese were successful in robbing them of life, liberty and the pursuit of happiness. Those sailors would never return home, never kiss mama again. Some of them would never start a family or see the wives and children they left behind. The media showed a weak enemy. Those sailors witnessed a powerful and dangerous adversary, willing to stop at nothing to kill them. They couldn't see what everyone else in the world saw. They couldn't see victory.

I would like for us as Christians to draw some parallels. Let's begin with some questions. In the eternal battle between good and evil, which is more powerful: God's all-encompassing love and perfect will or Satan's schemes and lies? Who will be the victor? If you answered "God," congratulations for you are correct. Do you really believe that? If so, it's time for us to stop acting defeated. It is time for us to recognize and combat the evil in this world for what it truly is.

To get a little perspective, we can look all the way back to Hebrew tradition, which tells us that one-third of the angels fell from Heaven with Satan. Although it is not mentioned specifically in our scripture, most Bible scholars look to Revelation 12:4 for evidence of this. It states **"His tail swept away a third of the stars out of the sky and flung them to earth."** That's an impressive feat pulled off by a charismatic leader. He convinced 33% of the angels hovering around God's throne, continually basking in His glory, relentlessly stating His awesomeness by constantly, according to Isaiah 6:3 **"...calling to one another: 'Holy, holy, holy is the Lord Almighty; the whole earth is full of his glory.'"** Satan broke off a sizable chunk of God's warriors and convinced them to follow him. Powerful. Scary even. 1 Peter 5:8 refers to him as a dangerous **"roaring lion looking for someone to devour."**

Because of the schemes of this convincing general and his demon army, we've witnessed roughly 50 million legal abortions in this country in the past 40 years. According to the 2012 census, the state of Louisiana holds 4.6 million people. In other words, over 10 times the population of my home state has been aborted in this country over the past 4 decades.

We cannot seem to see past the media's portrayal of the "progress" being made by our society by allowing these abortions and other atrocities to continue. This is by no means our society's only shortcoming. I mention this one simply because of the abundance of data on it.

It's really easy for us to throw in the towel, retreat, and allow these things to happen. We cannot see out of the fog of war that envelopes us. We are witnessing a powerful enemy snatch our freedom, our children's innocence and our treasured beliefs away from us.

Why are all these terrible things happening? Because we, the Christians of this country and of this world, are acting defeated. Let's revisit the areas we've discussed. Satan convinced one-third of the angels to follow him. That means an army of two-thirds, double the size of what fell, remained. For every demon crawling this earth, there are 2 heavenly warriors. For every lie, there is a double amount of truth. The light overpowers the darkness 2 to 1. What does this mean for us? It means mathematically, we're ahead. Scripturally, we're going to win.

I believe what 1 Peter says when he calls Satan **"a roaring lion looking for someone to devour."** But, I can also tell you that

Revelation 5:5 tells us **"...Do not weep! See, the Lion of the tribe of Judah, the root of David, has triumphed."** This Lion of Judah is out there and he is infinitely bigger than this defeated, desperate, screaming lion and he's not hunting down someone to devour. He's beckoning those who need to be washed clean.

If we could see as our Father sees, if we could see through this fog of war in which Satan has enveloped us in, I'm convinced we would be amazed at the size of His family. If the spiritual iceberg were suddenly flipped upside down and exposed right there in the rude gaze of the public, the magnitude of the church He is building would literally render us speechless. We are given a glimpse of it in Revelation 7:9, which says **"I looked and there before me was a great multitude that no one could count, from every nation, tribe, people and language, standing before the throne."**

We as Christians are living between D-Day and V-Day. We are living between the D-day when Christ went to the cross and the final outcome was no longer in question and the V-Day when we will see Christ seated at the right hand of the throne of God. We are not defeated. **"No, in all these things, we are more than conquerors through him who loved us."** That came from Romans 8:37. Verses 38 and 39 go on to say, **"For I am convinced that neither death nor life, neither angels nor demons, neither the present nor the future, nor any powers, neither height nor depth, nor anything else in all creation, will be able to separate us from the love of God that is in Christ Jesus our Lord."**

In John 16:33, the Lion of Judah tells us, **"I have told you these things so that you may have peace. In this world, you will have trouble. But take heart. I have overcome the world."**

Satan is real. He is dangerous and he is alive. But, he is also defeated. Beginning today, as an individual, as a member of your family, and as a member of the body of Christ, I challenge you never to live defeated. Never accept the sin of this world as "that's just how it is." Lead a life that shows Satan who the victor really is. Recognize his attacks for what they are, the act of a defeated and desperate enemy. He knows there is no chance of victory so he and his demons attempt to slow down and frustrate the workings of the victor, Jesus Christ.

We are not defeated. No, we are more than conquerors.

Now, act like it.

The Isolated Christian

Have you ever noticed there seems to be something built inside each of us that tells us we don't need anybody else? In our culture today girls are taught to be strong, independent, and self-sufficient. Boys are encouraged to handle their problems quietly, internally and without emotion.

While this ideology is prevalent across the board of humanity, I'm reminded of an athlete I once heard say that he would have a great team except for all his teammates. People talk *team* but value *self*.

As Christians, we are not immune to this tendency. When this happens in our walk with Christ, the results are detrimental. It is called isolation. The people who are on this path usually claim to know the Bible and be a follower but usually do not attend church with any regularity. However, the faithful church-goer can have these problems as well. It has been my observation, that when asked about their behavior, these people usually ask the defensive question "Doesn't loving God come down to just me?"

The answer to that question is both yes and no. Yes, you need to love God with all *your* heart. No, you cannot do it alone. Don't fall into Satan's trap of isolation. Instead use the advice found in an African proverb I ran across. It says "If you want to go fast, go alone. If you want to go far, go together."

Isolation is one of Satan's most destructive weapons. Now, let's not get solitude and silence, which are two powerful disciplines, confused with isolation. Spending some time alone and remaining silent in order to hear God can be very beneficial and both are essential to a Christian's well-being. Isolation, on the other hand, is the prideful belief that you need no one in order to love God. This ignorant belief is the first step taken by the child of God on a downward spiral. First of all, if there are no other Christians around, there is no accountability. This absence leads to the gradual belief that there are no consequences for his or her actions.

King David held that mindset when he committed adultery with Bathsheba. She got pregnant and he had her husband killed and everything was perfect…until Nathan showed up. Nathan used a story to bring the sin that David's isolation gave birth to, to light.

In 2 Samuel chapter 12:1-7 Nathan said *"There were two men in a certain town, one rich and the other poor. The rich man had a very large number of sheep and cattle but the poor man had nothing except one little ewe lamb he had bought. He raised it, and it grew up with him and his children. It shared his food, drank from his cup and even slept in his arms. It was like a daughter to him. Now a traveler came to the rich man, but the rich man refrained from taking one of his own sheep or cattle to prepare a meal for the traveler who had come to him. Instead he took the ewe lamb that belonged to the poor man and prepared it for the one who had come to him." David burned with anger against the man and said to Nathan, "As surely as the Lord lives, the man who did this deserves to die. He must pay for that lamb four times over because he did such a thing and had no pity." Then Nathan said to David, "You are the man!"* Then he told him all the horrible things, including the death of his baby boy, that would take place because all sin has consequences. We may be forgiven, but the consequence still exists.

Accountability in our life as a Christian is a must. Even though the word "accountability" does not appear in the Bible, Jesus and his disciples modeled it constantly and there are many verses that reveal the value of this concept, including my favorite verse, Proverbs 27:17, which says *"As iron sharpens iron, so one man sharpens another."* When we look into the gospels, we find that Jesus did not send the disciples out by themselves. He sent them in pairs.

Having someone to hold you accountable is a blessing. This person is not here to point out your flaws or put you down. They are here to evaluate you, ask the tough questions, to keep you on the right path and to pray with you and for you. It is an essential part of my Christian walk to sit down with trusted brothers in the Lord and discuss things in my life and have them question me. First Thessalonians 5:11 says *"Therefore encourage one another and build each other, just as in fact you are doing."*

Think of it as a basketball game in the 4th quarter against a tough opponent where the 6th man comes into play. Who is the 6th man? The crowd. The cheering section. Their encouragement helps push the team to victory. Why do you think teams fear playing in LSU's Death Valley? It is not that the teams are that good. It's the loud, crazy, thundering, cheering crowds. Now, I'm an LSU fan and I'm so glad I can mention them in a Bible lesson but this is where our Christian life can learn something from the Fighting Tigers. Encouragement offered at the right time can be the difference between victory and defeat. So always be on the look-out for an opportunity to offer encouraging words and actions because we never know who we may encounter that may be on the verge of defeat. We need others and others need us.

Another step on the way down is that isolation leads to an end of the passion and the fire you felt for the Lord. Think of the embers in a fire. If you remove one of those and set it off by itself, it will immediately lose its orange color and begin cooling off. Soon it will be nothing but a black, charred, worthless piece of wood. All the while, the pile of coals is still going strong. By surrounding ourselves with other Christians and sharing what God has done for us and hearing others share their stories, we are blessed and our appreciation and need for God is increased. In isolation, we never hear the good news of God's moving and shaking in the lives of others, and eventually God's grace seems irrelevant.

Never feel that you can go at the Christian life alone. We must depend on each other to keep us from sin until the second coming. May we never turn our back on the brothers and sisters that the scriptures demand we consider. May we never let pride tell us we do not need anyone. May we never let fear keep us from confessing our sins. May we never keep quiet when God gives us a chance to encourage.

Don't be foolish and try it alone. Living the Christian life is a "we" thing, not a "me" thing. There is no such thing a Lone Ranger Christian.

The Famous Tractor
Incident of 2005

Murphy's Law. This universal truth roughly states: If it can go wrong, it will. However, there is a relatively unknown addendum to this rule known as the McNorton Corollary. This add-on, which could possibly be unique unto my family, alters the aforementioned law to state: If it can go wrong, it will at the precise moment to cause maximum financial damage and/or physical pain.

Many a time have I witnessed this natural truth enacted. Murphy's Law with the McNorton Corollary have appeared in such things as a busted outboard that waited for miles of swamp to pass before giving up the ghost, the crosshairs in a deer rifle's scope that decide to go haywire on a quick double-check the evening before season opens, or even a previously undetected yellow jacket nest in the grassy front yard that comes to resemble a miniature yet angry DFW airport when approached by a lawnmower. My point is pain and frustration are always lurking. When they decide to attack, you remember.

Now, all laws by definition are solid, binding, explainable, provable truths. While Murphy's Law and the McNorton Corollary both make cameo appearances in this tale, there is one part that no amount of science or study can explain. On with the story:

In the late spring of 2005, my father and his older brother decided to get their 1972 model Kubota tractor in shape for the upcoming mowing season. The previous winter had the left the tractor's battery with about as much punch as a shoebox, so a pull-start was deemed necessary. Their houses sit on a long stretch of flat, straight dirt road that runs parallel to the banks of Black Lake. So, they hooked that relic up to a diesel pick-up using a chain. My Uncle Johnny hopped into the truck, my father got on the tractor and away they went. However, when they reached the end of the flat section of road, the ol' fossil had yet to fire. Now, they had a decision to make. To their left was a 90-degree turn which led to more flat straight road. Directly ahead of them lay one of the steepest hills in this part of the country. I am willing to bet you can guess which route they chose.

For reasons unbeknownst to me, up the big hill they went. The best I can figure is they were hoping the time-worn tractor's engine would turn over on the way up the hill. Then, they could unhook it from the truck, ease it back down the hill and they would be good to go. However, when they reached the hill's zenith, the motor had yet to show signs of life. It was at this particular juncture that they gave Murphy's Law ample room to show up and show out.

There they sat on top of the big hill with a dead antique tractor hooked to the back of a noisy diesel pickup truck. The tractor had to be brought home for these two men to determine the problem; therefore, leaving it on top of the hill simply was not an option. So, down the hill the pickup-pulled tractor came with my father perched atop. Everything with the return trip was going fine until my father looked down and noticed there was slack in the chain. The inert tractor was slowly but surely gaining on the truck. My father tried to rectify the situation by applying the brakes. While the decrepit brakes did slow the tractor a bit on its gravity-induced descent, my father felt he may need to exert more force on the brake pedal to improve its function. For leverage, he pulled upward on the tractor's steering wheel to help him push the pedal down harder. If it can go wrong, it will at the precise moment to cause maximum financial damage and/or physical pain. This was that moment.

The steering wheel popped off in his hands, thereby making my father the unwilling passenger on this rusty rollercoaster. Unable to flag down his hard-of-hearing brother over the rattling diesel truck engine and surmising a jump was inevitable, he prepared to bail. Not wanting to end up as a hood ornament on this careening jalopy, he ensured his feet were free for the dive and then waited to see which direction the tractor had decided it should go. Shortly, it became obvious that the tractor had its heart set on the right-hand ditch. My father waited to be sure and then leapt from the left side of the tractor.

The tractor did end up propped up against the dirt embankment on the right-hand side of the road. However, no amount of reasoning or contemplation can explain where my father came to rest. When he exited the vehicle, he was bound for the left-hand ditch. However, after he landed on his head, neck and shoulder, he found himself, complete with a torn and partially detached retina in his right eye and a concussion, lying in a pile of dust on the *right-hand* side of the road. To this day, he has no clue or in what manner he managed to clear the tractor and chain, all apparently in mid-air. All he knows is that he did.

After finally putting this tale on paper, I do not know which axiom better describes one man pulling a dead, crusty tractor down a gravel hill with his brother perched atop it best: Murphy's Law of things going wrong and causing damage even if it defies physics or the eternal words of the renowned philosopher Forrest Gump, "Stupid is as stupid does."

Storms of This Life

Job 1:1-8 says, *In the land of Uz there lived a man whose name was Job. This man was blameless and upright; he feared God and shunned evil. He had seven sons and three daughters, and he owned seven thousand sheep, three thousand camels, five hundred yoke of oxen and five hundred donkeys, and had a large number of servants. He was the greatest man among all the people of the East. His sons used to take turns holding feasts in their homes, and they would invite their three sisters to eat and drink with them. When a period of feasting had run its course, Job would send and have them purified. Early in the morning he would sacrifice a burnt offering for each of them, thinking, "Perhaps my children have sinned and cursed God in their hearts." This was Job's regular custom. One day the angels came to present themselves before the LORD, and Satan also came with them. The LORD said to Satan, "Where have you come from?" Satan answered the LORD, "From roaming through the earth and going back and forth in it." Then the LORD said to Satan, "Have you considered my servant Job? There is no one on earth like him; he is blameless and upright, a man who fears God and shuns evil."*

I want you to imagine for a moment that you are in a very crowded place like an auditorium and the person on stage just asked for a volunteer. What would you do? Would you spring from your seat, arms waving wildly, all the while screaming "Pick me! Pick me!" or would you sink down in your seat and pretend to be tying your shoe until the volunteer was selected and you felt it was safe to resurface?

In the matter of a few seconds, I have divided all of the Earth's population into 2 basic groups. First, there are those who crave the spotlight and, when given the opportunity, jump for it. Then, there is everybody else. The majority of the population wishes that they could become invisible when such an offer is extended.

I can't help but feel that Job, like most of us, would have fit nicely into group number 2. The first 5 verses of the book that bears his name tell us of his wealth, family, occupation and daily rituals and habits. He was just minding his own business doing the best he could with all that he had been blessed with. Then, God had to go off and call him out to center stage "right there in the rude gaze of the public" as my grandmother would say. God called him to Satan's attention. And if that weren't enough, God went on ahead and offered him up as a bombing range for Satan's attacks. I can't help but imagine that if Job had been privy to this conversation, he might have had an objection or two.

Now, if you know anything about the story of Job, you know his trials were severe. In a matter of moments, he sees his wealth, security, and children vanish followed shortly by a quick deterioration of his health.

How many of us have ever experienced a trial or storm in this life?

We all have. Have we ever noticed how we are experts at our own suffering? Ever notice how we specialize our sufferings to bring out the worst in them to show how uniquely terrible they are? If you read my first book, you know that I suffer from a rare condition with my eyelids that causes them to involuntarily close for long periods of time. I could read Job's story and say "That's terrible, but at least he kept his eyesight." Others could say "At least he didn't have to bury a spouse or endure divorce." Or "At least he had friends nearby." You see, we are experts at our own agony.

But, as we study Job's story, we see he never lost his faith or his integrity. Do we believe that maybe--just maybe-- God has allowed the trials and storms to enter your life because He trusts your faith and He knows your strength, like he did Job's?

If our trust is truly and firmly in Him, then these storms will have the ability to blow away all cluttering doubt and leave us with a new wisdom useful in counseling others along with an unflinching, unwavering hope and peace that surpasses all human understanding.

Through every storm, every trial, Jesus is right there every step of the way providing-- not an answer or an explanation--but a comfort through His word, through His presence and through His people, all the while showing us a way out.

1 Corinthians 10:13 says, ***"No temptation has seized you except what is common to man."*** Nothing has seized you, nothing has happened to you except what is common to man. In others words, your trials, your storms, as awful as they may be, are nothing new. Like the sign I once saw at a cashier's register said *"You are special. Just like everybody else."*

Now, I'm a math teacher by trade so I have some numbers to throw at you. This condition I have, known as blephrospasm, affects 1 out of every 20,000 people in the United States. There are roughly 314 million people in the U.S. That means that there are nearly 16,000 people living with this condition in the U.S. today, which would average 320 per state. So, it's not that rare. It's not even unique in my own family. My great uncle also was diagnosed with it.

Was your family torn apart by divorce? So were the families of 87,221 other people last year alone. Was your life turned on its head when you lost your job last year? You are in the same boat with 7.5 million other U.S. citizens.

My point is as Christians, we are never alone. We are never in this by ourselves. We have each other and above that we have our

Christ. To the non-believer, this is not true. It's simply them versus the world (aka Satan's stronghold).

When, not *if*, we face the trials and storms that this life will throw at us, pray. Pray for strength that only God can provide. Pray for peace which surpasses all human reasoning. When we are called out to center stage to publicly endure heartbreak or loss, ask God to bless you with what you'll need to be that man or woman of Christ that He needs you to be during this entire ordeal.

And above all remember this: all the storms and tribulations of this life must pass through His hands first.

A Bit of Smoke (and other random thoughts on James)

If we reduce all scriptures to their basic common denominator, we will find two prevailing themes:

1. The way to God--written to the lost, includes the plan of salvation
2. The walk with God--written to believers, how to live like a Christian

The book of *James* definitely falls into the second category. It was written to believers *"scattered among the nations"* (1:1). "Scattered" here in the Hebrew language is similar to how a farmer would scatter seed. These Christians were the ones scattered after Stephen's death. One thing I have learned about *James* is that it was not meant to be a comforting, cuddly bedtime story. It was designed to convict, not to comfort.

James has been referred to as many different things. One was a burr under the saddle. Nowadays, horses are not our main source of transportation so a different version would be a grain of sand in a oyster. Uncomfortable, irritating (because no one likes his or her flaws being pointed out especially with the raw efficiency that James does it), but it eventually produces a pearl of wisdom and guidance.

I heard a wise old preacher say "You don't preach on *James*, you pick which part of *James* you want to preach." Numerous topics and challenges are crammed into these five brief, yet powerful chapters. So, I will not attempt to discuss this epistle in its entirety as I believe that could be a book unto itself (pun intended). However, I would like to discuss the parts where Jesus' little brother has convicted and challenged me personally.

James dedicates nearly all of chapter 3 to discussing the dangers of the tongue. He refers to it as *"a very small part of the body, but it makes great boasts."* He also calls it *"a restless evil full of deadly poison"* in verse 8 of chapter 3. James pulls out all the stops when dealing with this subject. He realizes how unruly a tongue can be when he says in verses 7 and 8 *"All kinds of animals, birds, reptiles, and creatures of the sea are being tamed by men, but no man can tame the tongue."*

Speaking from personal experience, nothing can damage your Christian appearance and ministry faster than a slip of the tongue. Nothing can ignite anger faster or can break hearts more efficiently than the tongue.

From now on, we should make it a point to be like the preacher who was always in a good mood praising the Lord for something each day. The one cloudy, rainy, Sunday morning the ceiling leaked and ruined the piano and soaked the pews. Then a water pipe burst and flooded the basement. During that day's service, he thanked God that every day was not like this.

Can you remember asking someone how they were doing and regretting it a few seconds later? I certainly can. I was just trying to make friendly conversation. After I got a sob story complete with their list of ailments, I walked away a bit depressed. But on the other hand, I can also remember asking one elderly lady who was a substitute teacher how she was one day. She had to use a cane to get around. Her car appeared to be held together by the Holy Spirit and she survived on unpredictable substitute teacher's pay. But in spite of all that, she answered me, even with a frail voice, without hesitation, "I'm blessed. How are you?"

I learned an important lesson that day. As children of God, we should always be able to tell someone how great we are doing. If we can't do that, then we can tell them how great we are about to be doing. Use the tongue to spread the good news. Tell somebody how blessed you are. Then tell them how you got that way. Satan has enough tools. Don't give him your tongue, too.

Chapter 4 of *James* houses a candid reminder of the brevity of life. Verses 13 and 14 state: ***"Now listen, you who say, 'Today or tomorrow we will go to this or that city, spend a year there, carry on business and make money.' Why, you do not even know what will happen tomorrow. What is your life? You are a mist that appears for a little while and then vanishes."***

How long does a mist or a fog hang around? It never hangs around once the sun gets up high enough to burn it off. That is what James compared our lives to here on Earth. I have always enjoyed the version that refers to our lives as "a bit of smoke." One gust of wind and it is gone forever. In my 11 years in the classroom, I have been reminded of this harsh fact. I have stood by the graves of more of my students than I ever imagined I would.

Our lives are marked by uncertainty. From the cradle to the grave we are at the mercy of our surroundings. We are never so powerful to avoid failure, never so rich to avoid being in need, never so secure to avoid needing prayer.

So, we need to make plans for our future with God in mind. Too many times we make plans as if God does not exist. I could ask you where you are going to be ten years from now and I would probably get a solid, rehearsed answer. This is good. But how would you react if God steps in and rearranges your plans? I never planned on leaving my classroom. I certainly never dreamed of being a full-time author or youth minister. But, one case of blephrospasm later and here I am.

Walking with God gives us perspective about what we really are. It doesn't guarantee we will live longer, but it does help us live a better, deeper, broader life. Since we, as mere humans, do not know what the hour, day, week, month or year that lies before us will bring, we should commit ourselves anew to the One who does know.

When we do that, no matter what we are dealt, we know it is within the Lord's will. We know we are living for him. And that is the greatest life anyone could ever dream of.

Depend on God.
Trust His Will.
Honor His Word.

P. S.

Thank you. Thank you for your time and your support. I never dreamed my dusty old stories would ever comprise a book, much less two of them. I never dreamed that I would be considered an author, yet here I am. Through this metamorphosis, I have learned that if you are still moving air, God is not through with you. Even if our lives here are about as permanent as *A Bit of Smoke*, God can use our time here to bless others for an eternity. I have prayed for you. I have asked God to challenge you, to give you the desire to examine yourself and to see what you will leave behind. What you are going through right now will become part of your story. Remember the parts that need to be told.

God bless,
Ben Dupree

Email Ben at <u>bendupree00@gmail.com</u> for upcoming events and to book speaking engagements. Like his page "Ben Dupree-author" on Facebook or follow him on Twitter @bendupreeauthor for all the latest on book signings and releases.

Printed in the United States
By Bookmasters